THE UNDERGROUND GUIDE TO CLASSROOM MANAGEMENT

Connor McGill

This book is dedicated to all the teachers who have the guts to get up each and every day to teach their hearts out.

Table of Contents

WHO AM I?

Great question. What gives me the credentials to write this guide? I'm a veteran teacher. I have been, and still am, in the trenches teaching my heart out every day. I believe 18, going on 19 years of service in a tough school gives me the right to call myself a veteran. It is said at my school, "If you can teach here, you can teach anywhere." And that's the truth. I've seen people come and go. Some get chewed up and spit out. Others stay, tough it out, take their lumps, and learn how to survive and thrive.

I'm writing this under a pen name. Why? I want to tell the truth, and I want to keep my job. I'm tired of phony administrators who may have taught in the classroom 3 or 4 years telling teachers how to do their jobs or writing how-to manuals (Luckily, I've had the good fortune to work under 4 great principals). No, I'm not bitter—I only have the desire for teachers to have a different way of thinking. A real-world approach as opposed to a scholarly, out-of-date, politically correct method. I know what works. I know what doesn't. The pen name gives me the freedom to tell it like it *really* is.

I teach over 600 different students a week as a special areas teacher in an elementary school. Like I mentioned before, it can be a rough place at times. I may not have seen it all, but I have experienced a lot and want to teach you how to control your classroom with confidence.

I believe teachers are special people and I have witnessed too much frustration and I've seen good people leaving the profession early because they couldn't figure out classroom management. We all got in to teaching to teach—not to correct behavior. Let's get these kids in line and get back to teaching.

I'm going to give you about 50 things to think about. You can read the book out of order and it will still make sense. This isn't a 300 page book with a bunch of filler that in the end doesn't say much of anything. I've read plenty of those. I've actually been working on this guide off and on for the last 7 years. You'd think after 7 years that it'd be 7,000 pages long but it's not. As a teacher myself I know you're busy and I cut anything out that I thought would be a waste of your time. I envisioned this guide as something you could pick up, read a chapter within a few minutes, and then think about how you could use the idea in your classroom. Then, read another later and chew on that for a bit. Or read it all at one time. Whatever works for you. I hope you find some helpful ideas.

Please take these strategies and make them your own by adding your style and personality.

I want you to enjoy teaching like I do.

WHO'S THE BOSS?

Who is the boss in your classroom? Are the kids in control or are you? Let's imagine your classroom as a pack of dogs (some days it probably feels that way). Dog packs have an alpha dog. Are you the alpha dog in your pack? It all starts with you. It all starts with a mindset.

Be the alpha dog. I *know* that I'm the alpha dog in my room. No, I'm not a bully. I love my students dearly, but they need a leader and that's me. That is my responsibility. Without a clear voice of leadership there will be chaos, and chaos only breeds frustration and more problems.

As soon as my students walk through the door to my room, my "reign" begins. I'm the King (or you can be the Queen). I don't want you to think that you have to rule with an "iron fist." It is more of a "tough love."

I will state this one more time because I think it is so important. I love my students. If you make your decisions with love, your decisions will be right. If you make your decisions and policies with frustration and anger, I can almost guarantee you that they will fail.

So, how do you become the alpha dog? First, you have to realize that the students are not your friends. It would certainly be great if they thought you were a great and fascinating person, but at the end of the day—you're their teacher, not their friend.

As an art teacher in a very large school, I teach 6 classes a day, 30 classes a week. I get the unique opportunity to see how 30 different teachers lead their classes. Teachers who try to be too friendly with their classes almost always fail. Children need structure and rules. They actually like them and feel safe when they have boundaries. If you need friends—join a social club. Do the students a favor and be their teacher, not their friend. Be the alpha dog.

Think of the classroom as a social structure with you at the top—the pack leader. You will be tested! That is the natural way of the pack and your job is to nip all the problems in the bud. Be dominate, yet calm and assertive. To be dominate does not mean to be cruel, harsh, angry, or bossy. Nobody wins with this type of leader. Instead, stay peaceful, stay kind, and stay firm. Set rules and expect them to be followed. Set boundaries and expect them not to be crossed. You want students to respect you—not fear you.

PROCEDURES, PROCEDURES, PROCEDURES (HUP, TWO, THREE, FOUR)

At the beginning of each year I feel like a drill sergeant when it comes to procedures. We practice walking in the door. We practice sitting down. We practice getting supplies out and putting them back up. We practice lining up—and on and on. If the class does not do it right, the class does it again. Yes, it can be incredibly boring at times, but the payoff is worth it. Students like routines and feel safe in a predictable environment.

Practicing procedures establishes within the psyche of the class that you mean business. Don't let them slip! If you let the students slip once, they will take note of it and try you again. If you *never* let them have a free-pass, the class will quickly learn that it is just easier to do it your way.

I am aware that it is not always practical to stop what you're doing and practice something. If the class is lining up to get on the bus and go home and the students push and shove, it would not be appropriate to make the busses wait or have the students miss the bus while you practiced lining up. So, I give myself an out when establishing the rules. I state that if the class does not perform a certain task correctly, it is my choice as the teacher to either do it again or give a consequence.

For example: When students come into my art room, my rule is to come in without talking and sit down. As I write this chapter I am in the sixth week of the school year. The classes that do not follow this rule go back out, line up outside the room, and come in again. After the second or third week of school it is rare that we have to do this. Today, I needed every second of class time to review and finish a project. As the students were coming in, I heard a few people talking and simply announced that the class owed me 5 minutes of silence once the lesson was complete and they were in their seats (the students are usually allowed to whisper as they work). After I made the announcement they were silent, sat down, and I was able to quickly review and get them working. The consequence as opposed to practicing was no surprise to the students as I clearly explained this to them earlier.

On a side note: If students were to continue talking after I announced the 5 minutes of silence, I would add another minute or give individual consequences. When adding minutes, if the class ever gets to ten minutes—I have a special set of consequences. More on consequences later.

As for now, practice really does make perfect. It's worth it.

ARE YOU THE PROBLEM?

So, how do you do all of this? It sounds great, huh? Believe me it is. My daily life in the classroom was sometimes a living hell my first couple of years. I wanted to quit. I wanted out. I was thinking about doing anything other than teaching the monsters. But, I didn't. I made a decision to stay and to learn.

I had to look at myself first and then I had to re-examine every part of my school day. I scrutinized everything. I put on my Mr. Fix-It hat and began tearing apart everything and putting it back together because I realized that one of the biggest problems I had was me.

I have a lot of hobbies and I'm a night owl. My muse seems to enjoy visiting when the sun goes down and the closer it gets to midnight the louder I can hear her voice. My first two years of teaching were done with very little sleep. Sometimes I was just making it through the day so I could get home, take a nap, and then repeat my cycle.

During my first two years I also would enjoy a few adult beverages most nights. If the mornings weren't hard enough after staying up until midnight, add a slight hangover to it and my mornings were torture.

I wasn't setting myself up for success. The students were terrible because I left the door open for them to goof off. I wasn't focused and my classes suffered.

I was a huge part of the problem. I learned that I have to turn out my light and go to sleep before 11pm. I actually have a pretty steady routine where I get in bed at 9:30 and read until 10:40 if I can make it that long. I get a good night's sleep. On the weekends I stay up late and on holidays and breaks. I've finally learned that staying up late to play with my Muse is just not worth it or fair to the students I teach.

Another problem I had was not being prepared. I learned if I had to stop and cut paper or get this or that together, I'd lose them. These days I'm organized and always prepared. I don't open the door for mischief.

I was the problem.

Is there something you do that needs to change?

STRAIGHT TALK

When I first started teaching I had a hard time being blunt with students. I didn't want to hurt their feelings. I was always beating around the bush. After a few years I learned that hitting someone with the truth is always best.

Bang. It's powerful.

When it comes to behavior I'm blunt. When I began my career it was so hard for me to correct the behavior of cute little girls. In my mind they were adorable and fragile. In reality they were wolves in sheep clothing. They ran all over me until I finally decided enough was enough. I can now look a cute 5-year-old with pigtails in the eyes and say, "I'm disappointed with you. I expect better. You *can* do better, and you *will* do better."

And then the tears start. I know I hit a nerve. I got through to that student. Again, straight talk does not mean you're talking out of anger and being cruel. It is telling it like it is. The truth.

When I first started teaching I worried that kids wouldn't like me if I said what was on my mind. I got over that, but I also realized that 99% of them will like you even if you give them a heavy dose of the truth. It still amazes me how I can get on to a kid in my classroom, and then see them in the hallway or cafeteria a couple hours later and they're so happy to see me with a giant smile and a wave.

This isn't about behavior, but I had a student run up to me to show me his artwork. I'd given the project details about 5 minutes before. The project should've taken at least 2 class periods. He was so proud he finished first. I looked at it and said, "I'm sorry but this isn't good. Usually, the person who finishes first does the messiest work. Good work takes time. Would you want me to hang this by the front door of the school with your name on it?" He shook his head. I'm sure it hurt his feelings. I said it with kindness. It came from a good place. It's not easy to hurt someone's feelings. Since then he's taken his time. I may have done this kid a huge favor by being blunt.

Kids are resilient—they can handle the truth, so give it to them.

IT'S A REPETITIVE JOB (YES IT IS, YES IT IS)

"I'm looking to see if your feet are on the tape. I'm looking to see your arm choice—folded, by your side, or in your pockets. And I'm listening to hear that voices are off."

I say this 6 times a day, Monday through Friday. And this is just when we line up. I have specific things I say when we clean up, when students enter the room, and when I'm not happy with the noise level. Teaching school is an extremely repetitive job.

Teaching behaviors is repetitive. It's boring. But it works.

My students know what I expect when they're lining up. We do the same thing every time.

When my students enter the classroom I like them to do it silently. Rule number one on my list is Enter Silently. I think it sets the stage for a good class. I remind some students every week of this rule. Every week.

I say and do some of the same things over and over again. It's the nature of the job.

By the end of the year I see some of my students mouthing the words I'm saying as I say them. The words don't change. They are the same every time.

Most jobs are repetitive. Cashiers ring up item after item. The guy or gal at the oil change place drains oil and replaces it all day long. It serves a purpose. The teacher teaches and unfortunately a lot of that teaching has to do with behavior.

Over and over, and over again.

THE RULES

1. Enter Silently
2. Raise your hand
3. Whisper while you work
4. When I talk – you stop talking

These are my four rules. Short and to the point. Yours of course will be different. If you teach math you might not want whispering during work time. I display the rules above the white board and refer to them all day long. If the class has moved away from whispering I say, "Rule number 3 says, 'Whisper while you work.' This is not whispering." When a student calls out during the lesson I say, "Rule number 2 says, 'Raise your hand.'" I point to the rules hanging on the wall.

I've been in classrooms with 10 or more rules and lengthy sentences describing what they are. The shorter the better. When we go over the rules at the beginning of the year it never fails that somebody will say, "It doesn't say no hitting." The rules can't say everything. Some things are understood. We respect each other—we're kind.

Maybe I should add one more.

5. Be kind.

Done (Nothing is ever set in stone).

BRING THE ENERGY

I stand at the door as my classes enter the room. I try to acknowledge each and every student. It may be something as simple as eye contact, a nod of my head, or a wink. With this simple gesture, each student knows that I know they're there. Do you ever remember feeling like a teacher didn't even know you were alive? I do. I didn't work as hard for that teacher.

Can this method be tiring? Yes. Does it take a lot of energy? Yes. But once again, it's worth it. Kids are worth it. Remind yourself every day why you are doing what you're doing. It certainly isn't for the money.

After my students start working at their tables I take a walk around the room and give praise. Praise is an incredible motivator. I might tell somebody how much I like something they're doing. I might give a thumb's up or a touch on a shoulder. Maybe just a look. But, everybody knows that I know they exist.

I spend a great deal of energy on the students with the worst behaviors. I try to get to know them the best. I sit at their table while they're working for conversation. When I see them in the hall I make a point to catch their eye and say hello. I have lunch with them on occasion and have them help with special projects.

One year I had a student that was full of hate. He hated his classroom teacher, all the kids in the room, the school, and me. I invited him to have lunch with me every Friday. We had lunch and talked and then I taught him how to use tools as we fixed things around the room and the building. I have to admit that most Fridays I didn't want to do it. I was tired from the long week and getting this kid to talk was painful. The first few Fridays I talked and he stared at me sizing me up. The silences were long and our 45 minutes together felt like hours. He probably thought I would give up on him, but I didn't. I wanted to because it was hard—but I didn't.

We had lunch together every Friday for two years. When we ran out of things to fix I broke things just so we could put them back together. He finally started talking to me. I could make him laugh. He trusted me. We never had any amazing break-throughs where he became the world's best student, but he was good for me. He never gave me any prob-lems. I don't know what happened to him or where he is today, but hopefully he will remember that someone took the time, put in the energy, and made him feel like he was worth it.

That's all I can hope for. I'm glad I spent that energy on him.
Every kid is worth it, no matter how unlovable they might at first seem.

Bring the energy.

BE A DETECTIVE

As a teacher you are also a detective. We have no idea what a kid goes home to when they get on the bus and leave the school. Whatever happens at home makes all kids different. They might get tons of love at home or they might get none. They might go home to kindness or they might go home to anger and someone cruel. We as teachers are left at a disadvantage in this regard. We don't know what happens at home.

Because of their upbringing, all kids will not respond to the same things. A direct tone with one student may correct a behavior when with another it might make them cower in a corner. You have to be flexible in your approaches. One size fits all does not work when it comes to classroom management.

In my early years of teaching I once threatened a class that they would have to clean the spider webs out of the windows if they kept up with their poor behavior. They collectively cheered. They wanted to do it. I remember being pretty stunned. One of the worst kids in the class came up to me later and said he loved to clean and really wanted to clean the windows. I told him I was just kidding about the windows but if he was good I would let him sweep at the end of class. He wasn't perfect but he was pretty good. Who knew a broom and a dustpan were so exciting?

I've found a lot of kids with challenging behaviors over the years who like helping out around the room. I discovered a little girl who was nothing less than a holy terror loved to organize things. She organized my spools of yarn, separated construction paper in different colored stacks, and rearranged my desk. I messed things up so she could clean.

I've never bought a student anything. No popcorn parties, no popsicles, no pencils or special erasers. Nothing. Nada. Zilch. There are things that are much more valuable than material items. You just have to figure out what they are. At my school the kids love soccer. I overheard a group of boys talking about how they could beat the fifth graders if they had a better goalie. I asked if I could be their goalie and their eyes lit up. Yes—they wanted me in goal. We set down the parameters of what they had to do to earn this and to make a long story short the fourth-grade boys (plus me) beat the fifth-grade boys.

Another time I had a fifth-grade girl who was challenging and by listening and trying to figure her out I discovered she was into track and considered herself the fastest person in the school. I assured her

I could beat her in a race and she just laughed in my face. I told her I was serious, but I would only race her if she did her work and didn't give me any trouble for 3 classes in a row. I didn't know if she would bite on the challenge, but she bit. After her third week of good behavior I met her at recess and the kids all gathered around because word had spread about the race. I won by a hair and got three more weeks of good behavior when she requested a rematch. I gave it everything I had but I was just getting over my shin splints and she won the second round. She was never perfect for me, but she was much better. We had connected on a different level.

Every kid has something you can connect with. A TV show you both like. A food. A sport. Music. Something you both fear. There *is* a connection—you just have to find it.

Be a detective.

JUST SHUT UP

Sometimes I just have to bite my tongue because I want to be nasty. Anger swirls through my body and my mind fizzles. Sparks are most probably flying out of my eyes. If I allow my tongue to move in these moments I'm probably going to get myself in trouble. A.k.a. fired.

Times like these are perfect for practicing your evil teacher stare. I put on my most evil face (I don't have to try very hard as I feel as if Satan himself has come to my body for a visit) and I freeze. I don't blink. I grit my teeth. I clench my fists. And I scream in my head all the foul things I desperately want to come out of my mouth. I don't allow them to do that because I for the most part love my job and my family needs the health insurance.

I learned this skill in the first few years of my marriage. As is my usual pattern for learning things, I learned the hard way. I spent a lot of time in the doghouse. Some things are meant to be thought and not said. I got married during my first year in the classroom so I soon found out that this skill I learned at home can be just as valuable at school.

I had a stare down, scream in my head event recently. I swear the kid could hear my thoughts because he looked terrified. The other students all got quiet and I could feel every eye in the room watching us. Like two gunslingers we faced off and waited for the other to make the first move. After I'd sweated him enough I slowly raised my hand with pointed finger and signaled for him to make his way back to where he belonged. All of this happened without a word.

When I'm teaching my lesson, I can oftentimes avoid having to stop and address behaviors with this same glare. An added eyebrow raise with the glare lets my intended target know who I'm looking at. If you haven't seen the YouTube video by Gerry Brooks on facial behavior management (Behavior Management Lesson 1), please watch it. He explains it better than I ever could.

Don't say those nasty things you really want to— you'll regret it.

ANOTHER NORMAL DAY (RULES DON'T CHANGE)

Every now and then something in your day will be different. In Georgia we sometimes have a two-hour delayed start to the school day because of ice. Or let's say half the class is out with lice—I know, gross, but it happens. And whenever something is different about the day the students all seem to think that the rules are going to be different.

I always go ahead and nip it in the bud and tell the students that the rules will be exactly the same. Even if it's a day or two before a holiday or break. Even if Halloween is on a week day. I know, I'm no fun. They moan and groan a bit and I'm sure they think horrible things about me, but that's okay, we have a normal class period and that makes me happy.

One year at the beginning of my career we broke up the classes for specials by the instruments they played in the band and orchestra. I'm not sure whose great idea this was but during one period I got the 7 percussion students while the other teachers had 30-35 kids in their classes. With the 7 percussion students I thought I had won the lottery. It was going to be the easiest class I had ever taught. Wrong. They were one of the worst groups I have ever had, and I don't mind saying that it was my fault. With such a small group I thought we wouldn't need rules, or a seating chart and I threw it all out of the window. And boy oh boy was I sorry. It opened my eyes to how invaluable the rules are to have in place and to use them no matter the class size or what's going on.

The rules are there for a reason. Don't give the students a reason to break them or they'll try it again.

IGNORE

If you grew up with a sibling you already know that sometimes you just did stuff to get under their skin. Students do this to us. I think it's almost like a sport to them. I remember a teacher in high school who had hearing aids. Kids would rub two quarters together under their desks to mess with his hearing devices. It drove him nuts. He certainly couldn't ignore this, but there are certain things as teachers we need to ignore to stay sane.

I have one student who hums to himself. It's not very loud and none of the other students are ever bothered by it. He does it so much that I don't think he even knows he's making any noise. If I ask him to stop he'll look at me quizzically and immediately go back to humming. It used to drive me nuts. It made my blood boil. How was this not driving everybody else crazy? So, I decided that I'd try to ignore it because no matter how many times I asked he never stopped. It really wasn't bothering anybody other than me. It still gets under my skin a little bit, but now I don't have to also deal with the frustration of him disobeying my instructions to stop the humming.

When we're cleaning up I give the class a few minutes to clean and then I count backwards from 10 to 1. When I get to 1 everybody is supposed to be seated, silent, and ready to go. For some reason, some kids in the class love to count with me and for some reason I hate that. No matter how many times I ask, somebody will still do it. Not every day. Not every class. But it happens enough that I had to sit myself down and decide if it was really something I should be getting bent out of shape about. So I decided to stop saying anything. I don't like that it happens, but it was a losing battle and not so important that I couldn't just suck it up and deal with it.

Is there something your students do that drive you a little bit crazy that you could just try to ignore? I know it's hard, but in the end it will save you the frustration of asking over and over and over again. In the end it will save you the extra annoyance of them *ignoring you.*

KNOW YOUR
AUDIENCE

I don't have a split personality, but I do act differently with each class. For some teachers, that might mean year to year, for me, it means hour to hour as I have 6 unique classes each day. I am basically a fun-loving person who enjoys using humor to get the students' attention. I am even pretty good at using different voices. Yes, I am one of those strange art teachers. Some classes can handle it, and some cannot. You have to know your audience.

One year I had a second-grade class who thought I was the funniest guy in the world (I am only mildly funny). The class was in stitches with every horrible joke I made. I really had to tone it down and be quite bland. It was hard, but my personality was affecting their behavior in a negative way. For a few weeks they asked me why I wasn't doing the funny voices or making jokes and I was honest and told them that they couldn't handle it. As the year went by I slowly tried to slip some of my personality back in and each time found out they were not mature or able to separate fun/silly time and serious/work time.

Is there something you may do, or not do that affects your students?

Some years the fifth-grade classes seem more mature than other years. I don't know how it works but some years they seem to know a lot about sexuality and other years nothing. It's weird. You have to know your audience. I'm not trying to be funny here, but you can avoid a lot of behavior problems by avoiding certain words. I have something I call practice clay I use when we're learning about ceramics. We practice different techniques with it and I collect it at the end of class. The students put the practice clay into a ball, put it in the middle of the table, and I collect it in a plastic bin. I'd been doing this for years and one time when I said what to do with the balls we had an amazing outburst. I haven't said it since. I knew this class was more advanced, but I wasn't thinking. I could have avoided the problem by knowing my audience.

I keep a close eye on which students can be near one another and which students cannot. One year I had two boys that no matter where I sat them, they would not leave each other alone. I tried to teach them how to ignore one another but they wouldn't. I ended up putting the boys on opposite ends of the room and I would pull a bookshelf out to block their view of one another. It was crazy but it worked.

In the same class I had two boys that would talk to each other no matter where I sat them. On the third week of class I pulled them aside and said, "Look, I'm going to put you two at the same table. I'll leave it this way as long as you're silent when I ask for silence and whisper when I ask for whispering. Can you do this?" They both nodded. I had to remind them every now and then of our agreement but it worked.

Get to know your audience and figure out what works best for the class.

ONE-ON-ONE

I've found out that kids aren't so tough when you get them one-on-one. Some of my students that can be real jerks in a group setting can be very different when you get them alone. There is no audience for them to impress and maybe, just maybe you'll have the opportunity to make a connection that will turn a really difficult kid into just a semi-difficult kid.

You do have to be careful about where you spend your one-on-one time. Being a man, I take extra precaution. I'm never in a room alone with a student without the door being open and sitting somewhere in the room in sight of anyone who walks past the door. Sometimes I'll meet a kid in the media center for a chat or we'll take a walk around the playground while the other kids are out playing. There are even a few benches out there that I use for my chats.

When I sit down for these little talks I'm not there to intimidate or to solve all the problems of the world; I'm there to open a dialogue. It's kind of like a peace offering. I'm there to get a kid to see me in a different light. I'm there to see them in a different light as well. We've all read the psychology textbooks that say some kids act out to receive attention. To them negative attention is better than no attention at all. Well, I'm there to give them positive attention. To listen. To talk about everything, or nothing, or something somewhere in between.

If you get a chance to do this I suggest you don't get preachy or reprimand. This isn't the time for that. If the student feels defensive you won't get anything out of them. They won't see you any differently and you'll only be beating your head against a wall. If they won't talk at first, tell them a little bit about yourself. Instead of asking them yes or no questions, ask them questions that require a more thoughtful answer. Teach them a game like checkers or chess.

Whatever you do, the secret here is to give them your full attention outside of the normal classroom environment. You'll be surprised how it will change their view of you, and their behavior.

ASSIGNED SEATS

After going over the rules and expectations for the year, this is the first thing I do—I assign seats. The kids say they hate it and they moan and groan, but I've tried it the other way and it doesn't work.

I have the students stand against a counter, which divides my room and I size them up. When the students go stand by the counter they oftentimes will stand right next to their best friend in the class. I can usually tell by simple observation if the two sitting next to each other will work or not. I don't always split them up. Sometimes putting them together makes things easier. I told the story in a previous chapter of the two boys I made a deal with who talked to each other no matter where I sat them. So, I put them next to each other and made a deal that they could be next to each other as long as they followed the rules.

I keep my assigned seating chart in pencil because it is constantly changing. I tell the students on the first day that I might move them in 30 seconds, 30 minutes, or next week. I tell them that if their seating assignment doesn't work out for any reason, they will be moved. I also point out the single desk I have in the room and tell them if I can't find a place where they can get their work done, they will be assigned to the single desk. Every now and then somebody gets assigned to that desk for a two week period (which is two classes) and then they get another chance. They rarely have to go back.

I never sit at my desk during class. I do have a stool at the end of the counter where I sit at times. From this spot I can see the entire room and there are two strategic spots on both sides of the counter where I assign seats to kids I want to keep a closer eye on. They look like every other seat and I am the only one who knows their significance.

Assigned seats won't win you any popularity contests, but you'll still come out a winner.

ANGER ISSUES

You are going to have students with anger problems. I give these students the space they need in the classroom. I have seats that by the normal eye look like the rest, but they actually have a wider buffer zone around them from the other students. I am gentle with these students and make sure they know it's okay to be wrong. When they make mistakes, I correct while I reassure them that they are still worthy, that I still believe in them, and that all people make mistakes. Being human is a messy job.

My school has two art teachers and the other art room is on the other side of the school. It's a big school. When I can tell one of my students with anger issues needs a breather I send him to the other art room for an errand. It might be to take a paint brush to the other art teacher or to borrow some blue paint. We've passed the same paint brush back and forth a dozen times. The other art teacher knows what I'm doing and she plays along.

Never meet anger with anger. I've tried it and it doesn't work. It will only create more anger. Teach tolerance and model level-headedness with your actions.

I teach a brother and sister who are in different grade levels. They're both angry bullies. I don't know this for a fact, but I'm guessing they live with an angry bully. It's what they know. I try to remind myself when dealing with them that they didn't grow up with loving, mature parents like I did. In the short time I have with them each week I have an amazing opportunity to show them how an authority figure *should* act. I don't let them off the hook. I don't look the other way and let them break rules because they'll get mad. I approach their anger with calm. I hold my ground with deep breaths reminding myself I'm not going to be drawn in with their anger. Some days it's hard as hell to do when all I want to do is unleash my tongue and rage. But I'm smarter than that. I've been there and down that road and know it will accomplish nothing.

Don't let your students' anger become your anger. Be the force that absorbs the anger and teaches that there is another way.

MAKE 'EM SWEAT

Sometimes to make a point with a student or class you have to make them sweat. If somebody has pushed me to the point where I'm going to give them a consequence, I might not tell them right away what it is. I want them to wonder what it might be. I want them to imagine the monster under the bed.

This is sometimes when the begging begins—when you've told them that they are in trouble (receiving a consequence, or however you like to phrase it). They will oftentimes even tell you the punishment they don't want. "Please don't call my parents." Or, "Am I going to miss recess?" And that's when I say I have to think about it. I tell them that it's too late to make the consequence go away, but the next 10-20 minutes (insert your own time-frame here) will help decide what is going to happen.

I mentioned before that I hate calling parents. It doesn't mean I won't throw the idea around. They don't know I don't want to do it. And I never lie about it. If I say I'm going to do it, believe me, I'll do it because nothing will sink you faster than empty threats. One of my favorite lines to use on them is, "Should I call your mom or your dad?" Watching their wheels spin is fascinating as they contemplate the question. The answer is usually, "Don't call either one." I don't let them off that easy. "Will your mom get mad if I bother her at work? Will that upset your dad?" I never commit to actually doing it. I'm just asking a few questions. Semantics.

Luckily the computer program I use to do report cards is tied to all of their personal information because 7 times out of ten the student will boldly tell me that I don't know their mom's phone number. I casually walk over to my laptop and in a few clicks of the mouse I tell them their address and all the numbers I have on file. I even politely invite them over to take a look. That usually shuts them up.

Fear of the unknown can be a good thing. Remember, don't ever be cruel—I don't want them to think I'm going to feed them to wolves or anything. They are children after all.

SOMETIMES YOU LOSE

I'm pretty darn good at classroom management. I'm a good teacher, but I'm an even better classroom manager. But, I can't solve every problem. Some problems don't have a solution. You have to realize that sometimes you can't win. There is not a cute success story in every tough kid. Some kids you just can't crack.

I've had this one kid for kindergarten, 1st grade, 2nd grade, 3rd grade, and 4th grade. He drives me absolutely nuts every year. When he comes to my art class it is the longest 45 minutes of my week—it feels like 3 hours. I don't hate anybody, but I almost hate this kid. Let's call it severe dislike.

None of my strategies work with this student. None of my tricks work. Nothing works. I just have to survive the 45 minutes and move on. This year I decided he was going to be my special project. I was going to have lunch with him, win him over, mentor him, take him under my wing, and do all the super special things I do to win over the tough kids. Nothing worked. He continued to be the biggest pain in my backside. He pushes every button I have that makes me go nuts. I can't figure him out.

I finally decided there is nothing to figure out. He just is like he is. I've heard his mother was addicted to drugs when he was born and I'm sure this has a lot to do with the way his brain is put together.

Some things are more powerful than a wily art teacher and his tried and true behavior strategies.

Sometimes you have to recognize that some things can't be overcome. You don't always get to win.

Sometimes you lose.

And that's okay.

UNSEEN FORCES

In the last chapter I talked about the kid with the drug addicted mother. It was just a rumor going around the school, but the important take away is that something was going on with that kid that we didn't know. Unseen forces were at work.

Every student has something unseen about them. Maybe they have multiple unseen things. I have two children of my own. One of my kids is happy-go-lucky and loves school. He even goes to school when he doesn't feel well because he loves it so much. My other kid is home schooled because she is afraid of failure. If she gets a 98 on a test she cries because she didn't get a 99. If she gets a 99 she cries because she didn't get a 100. To the casual observer she looks like a normal kid. She acts like a normal kid most of the time. But there are unseen forces at work. Her mother and I don't know where these anxieties came from, but they exist and they are real. (Update: After 3 years of homeschool my daughter came to us and said she wanted to give high school a try. She loves it. She's making good grades and even when she doesn't do as well as she hoped to do she doesn't freak out. My wife and I are absolutely perplexed. Unseen forces.)

I've had students come into my class who've always been wonderful turn into something completely different seemingly overnight. It's bizarre. Sometimes I find out why and most times I don't. It could be a new brother or sister on the way. A divorce or fighting between parents at home. A new boyfriend or girlfriend might have come in the picture for mom or dad. A new babysitter or afterschool program that the student doesn't like could be the case. They might have moved to a new apartment that is loud and they're not getting much sleep. The list could go on and on.

The important thing is to realize that there's probably a reason behind certain behaviors or changes in behavior. It's also important to know that we may never know what they are and that's just part of the job. Accept it and be mindful.

Teachers are surrounded by unseen forces.

A LINE IN THE SAND

My own children who are 13 and 14 years old were driving me absolutely nuts a few nights ago. My heart started pounding and my blood started to boil because they were ignoring me. They were rough housing upstairs and there's nothing wrong with a little roughhousing, but at a few minutes after nine at night I'm ready to settle down and it sounded like the ceiling was about to drop. As I marched upstairs I had it in my head to draw a line in the sand—one more episode of roughhousing would result in both of them losing their devices for two days.

My kids are not addicted to their phones and tablets, but they do adore them. A day without checking on their games or being able to contact their friends would be awful. It would definitely be a punishment that would hurt.

I asked myself as I marched up the stairs if I would be able to live up to my line in the sand. Before I got to the top I decided I would not.

If you draw a line in the sand with a student you have to make good on whatever you said. If you threaten to call a parent and they cross the line you have to call the parent. If you threaten an office visit, you have to send the student to the office. If a student crosses the line you've drawn and you don't make good on what you said, you lose all credibility, and they will do whatever they did again and again.

I hate calling parents. It's one of my least favorite things to do as a teacher. (You're probably getting tired of hearing that by now, but I'd rather spend an afternoon locked in a car with a rattlesnake) Early in my teaching career I used to use the threat of calling parents a lot. And, although I did make some phone calls, I didn't always make good on my threats. Do you think the students noticed? Of course they did. Every time the phone rang that night they probably wondered if it was me. When I didn't call they probably figured I'd forgotten. They won. I lost.

Don't draw a line in the sand unless you're ready to stick to your guns and follow through.

DON'T PLAY FAVORITES (TALK TO THE MEAN KIDS TOO)

This one is hard because we all have our favorite kids and the people we naturally gravitate toward. As my students are working I enjoy walking around the room and talking with them. There are some kids I could talk with all day. They make me laugh, we connect, and we have a good time being around one another. If you don't think other students notice this you're wrong. I've had students call me out on this in the past. And they were right, I was playing favorites.

As an art teacher, we do a lot of projects and the students work at tables with three or four other students. I present the lesson as they sit on the carpet. I have a white board where I can draw, show images from my computer, and more. After my lesson, they go to their tables and once they're settled I take my first trip around the room. On my first trip I try to start with compliments. Who doesn't love a compliment? And, I try to spend the majority of my time with students I don't know very well.

During testing a few years ago I was a proctor for a teacher who had a favorite. When I was in school we called it a class pet—I'm not sure if this term still applies. It was so obvious to me even after one day in her class that she adored this one child. Let's call the student Andrea. Andrea sharpened the pencils. Andrea passed out the papers. Andrea did this and Andrea did that. I was in the room testing for 5 days and by the end of the 5 days I almost hated Andrea. Can you imagine what the other students thought about her? I'm sure they hated her too. A lot of kids acted out while I was in there. Maybe they were trying to get some attention. Maybe they wanted some of what Andrea had. I wondered what would happen if this teacher had spread some of the chores around the room instead of having Andrea do every single thing. I wondered if some of her behavior problems would go away. I would bet that some of them would.

I have Andreas in all my classes—kids I love. Kids I would take home at the end of the day if it was okay. But I don't spend all of my time with these kids because it's not fair.

Talk to the quiet and mean kids too.

CONTACTING PARENTS

Calling parents is one of my least favorite things to do as a teacher. But, if it's done right it can be one of the most effective tools available to change the behavior of a problem student.

I have two of my own children and I received one of these calls when my son was in kindergarten. I immediately went on the defensive. So, knowing this I always open every call with a positive comment about the student and end the call with some form of praise. I slip all the negative stuff in the middle.

I don't think I'll ever forget one of the things my son's kindergarten teacher said to me on the call when I tried to defend him. He had not been turning in his papers, and the way he told it, she was the problem. She wasn't giving them time, he complained. When I told her this, she said, "If you'll only believe half of what he tells you about me, I'll only believe half of what he tells me about you." I could almost see her smile through the phone. I thought that was wise and I agreed.

I've had some productive phone calls that worked and changed behaviors, and I've had some where I was yelled at and told I didn't know what I was doing. I don't argue when I don't get the response I'm hoping for. I just think, "Well, that explains a lot" and move on. Sometimes the apple really doesn't fall far from the tree.

My music teacher friend across the hall doesn't mind calling parents. I don't think it bothers her at all. So, most of the time before she goes to make her phone call, she'll ask me if I'm having trouble with the same student. She is more than happy to tell the parent the trouble they're having in my class as well. Winning! We had trouble with the same kid a few weeks ago and she called his dad. His dad said to let him know if she had any more trouble with him. His dad said he'd take away his tablet for a couple of weeks. When I saw our shared student the next day he hadn't changed. I was happy to tell him that I knew about his dad's conversation with the music teacher. I was happy to tell him that I knew his dad wanted to know about any future trouble and what the consequence would be. I was happy when the unwanted behaviors stopped immediately. Thank heavens for my fearless music teacher friend.

If you aren't a big chicken like me—make the call.

THE A@#HOLE

Some kids just suck. And you know what—it's probably not their fault because if I was a betting man I would bet their parents suck too. But it is what it is and as teachers we have to play the cards we're dealt.

I once had a student who I'll call Chuck. Chuck strutted into my room each time with a swagger like he owned the place. He would look at me with disgust as if he'd been hoping I'd passed away since our last encounter and the realization that I was still alive was deeply disappointing. Chuck mumbled under his breath and although I never could quite understand what he was saying I'm certain he wasn't giving me compliments.

I was not fond of Chuck. Not even a little. He thought all my lessons were stupid. He thought my rules were ridiculous. I'm pretty sure my voice made his skin crawl. He hated everybody though and although it shouldn't have made me feel better it did. It didn't change the fact that he was an a@#hole.

My goal with these kinds of kids is to survive and

move on. You have to accept that you're not going to change them. You can certainly try, but it probably won't happen. Do your best to ignore their snide remarks. They're most certainly trying to get under your skin.

Don't let them turn *you* into an a@#hole.

REFLECT

I've found that sometimes the best way to solve current problems in the classroom is reflection. Recently I had a difficult student and an unusual situation. I will readily admit that I wasn't my best self. It bothered me. It bothered me because I'm good at classroom management. I take pride in how well I can run a classroom with very few problems. But I'm not perfect and I'm not immune to failure.

I let it go for the rest of the school day and moved on as dwelling on the problem and losing my focus for the day would only invite more problems. I didn't forget the situation, but I tucked it away to deal with later. I cleaned up the kitchen after dinner and the kids went off to their rooms to do homework. My wife was preparing for the following day at her job. I turned off the TV and put down my phone and replayed the encounter in my mind. I remembered what the student did. I recalled the hateful things he said. I remembered what I did and said. I thought about the way it made me feel. I tried to figure out what he was feeling as well. I watched it a few times in my memory. Then I put on my Mr. Fix-It hat and went through all of the things I should have done. I thought of all the things I should have said. I then imagined the edited version and tried to burn it into my memory. The next time I'm in a similar situation I hope to have a better approach. I hope to respond in a way I'm proud of with no regrets.

If you will view your job as a constant work in progress, I feel certain that you will be a better teacher. A teacher with a growth mindset has a better chance of making it 30 years than a teacher with a fixed mindset. I'm constantly learning and putting new "tools" in my teacher toolbox. Keep your toolbox open, no matter how long you've been teaching so you can add new tools along the way.

Reflect on your day. There's always room for one more approach to solving a problem.

SLACKERS

Some students need even more than a nod of my head or a kind smile. I have a student that has the ability to waste the whole period in dream-land while getting absolutely nothing finished. I've found that the more praise I give him, the better he does and the more he gets accomplished.

I give him a good pat on the back as he enters the room and a great big smile. As the students are getting settled into their seats, I make my first trip around the room with a quick stop at his table, and I find some way to compliment him. He eats it up. He wants to please me—and he has started getting most of his work finished. He even stops me when he sees me in the hall to tell me what he has been doing in his homeroom. I praise his effort some more.

I make more frequent stops at a slacker's table. When I notice they haven't done anything, I let them know I'll be back in 2 minutes and I want to see some progress. 2 minutes later I'll be back to check. They'll usually keep an eye on me as I'm walking around to see if I'm really coming back again. So, when I'm on the other side of the room I'll catch their eye if they're watching and I'll give them a look.

I've noticed that a lot of my slackers think they're not very good artists. I would imagine a good reason to slack off in math class or language arts would be the belief that you're not very good at those subjects. Since I don't lie to students, my trick for this is to praise their effort. Kids aren't stupid. They would probably know if I told them their artwork was great when it really wasn't. I can honestly say things like, "I like all the different colors you used. I like how you've tried to use all the different kinds of lines we've talked about in class. You're really trying hard and I'm proud of you."

Praise their efforts and I'll bet you'll get more of it with each passing day.

CONSEQUENCES

Unfortunately, when kids break the rules there have to be consequences. They don't have to be horrible or cruel to make them think twice the next time. The consequence just has to be something that sticks in their mind. You can even be creative. I was a camp counselor at an overnight summer camp that kids came to for a week at a time. I had a group of boys one week that would not stop talking and go to sleep. Part of the fun of summer camp is talking in your bunk after lights out—I get that, but these kids talked until two in the morning the first night. I wasn't having that. I said they could talk for 30 minutes and then they needed their sleep. It happened again the second night. The next day we had an hour scheduled at the pool and I told them we were going to be late. I hadn't seen any of them brush their teeth in the two days they'd been at camp. I told them to get their tooth brushes, tooth paste, and to meet me on the lawn in front of our cabin. I had them load up their brushes with tooth paste. I set a timer for 5 minutes, and they brushed. As they brushed I told them how important sleep was for counselors and campers and that if they talked past my 30 minutes again the brushing would be 10 minutes the next time and then 15 and so on. That night we all got a good night's sleep.

In the school setting my greatest weapon is to take away talking. Kids love to talk. I have a 3 strike rule in my room. Being an art class I allow my students to whisper as they work. If it gets too loud I say strike 1 to let them know the noise level is no longer acceptable. Strike 2 is a second reminder, and strike 3 is 5 minutes of silence. They hate it. If someone talks during the silence I add a minute onto the time remaining and they get an additional consequence (our school has a school-wide behavior system and they get a mark on what is called the clipboard). If we ever get to 10 minutes of silence we put away our art project and come back to the carpet to review the rules.

ADMINISTRATION (KEEP OUT!)

In every room in the school there is a button to push, which calls the office. If you need the assistant principal to come down and get an unruly kid out of your class you push the button and they come get the student. I pride myself on almost never pushing the button. I feel that pushing the button gives away all my power and tells the student that I can't deal with him or her.

Of course there are times when it is absolutely necessary. If there is a physical altercation I'm not going to sort it out in my classroom—it's an automatic office referral. But, other than that I try to solve *all* problems in my own room and not involve the administration.

I know some teachers who push the button as much as two or three times a week. They've let their class know that they don't know how to deal with their behavior. And, the student gets out of class. If their parents don't care if they get in trouble they might be doing this on purpose to get out of class. They get one-on-one attention from an adult. They get time away from the other students. I see it as the student getting a break and I'm not going to be a part of that.

Handle your own business as often as you can and the students will respect you more.

SHOW THEM YOU'RE HUMAN TOO

My son is in the eighth grade. I'm not bragging here, but he's a pretty smart kid. He's never made anything lower than an A on a report card. He told me last week that his Language Arts teacher has no soul. Guess which class he struggles in? (He's in danger of making the first B of his life) Yep—Language Arts. A lot of kids are people pleasers. My son is one of them, but he barely sees his Language Arts teacher as a person. I'd never heard him say he hated anybody before he met her. Maybe he's just being 13 and throwing the word around but in his mind he doesn't see her as human and he doesn't put any extra effort in his work for her class.

I've never met her so I don't know what the truth is. Maybe these are just the words of a junior high school boy. He did swear that she's never smiled. Not once in 5 months. Maybe she subscribes to the old teacher adage, "Don't let them see you smile until Christmas." I don't agree with that at all.

Show your students your personality. Let them know what you are interested in. Tell them about your family. Tell them about your pets and your hobbies. I don't tell the students my deepest dreams and desires but they know a lot about me and I try to find something to connect with each and every one of them. They know I'm married, have two kids, a cat, love Chinese food and doughnuts, and that I have written books (although I wouldn't really call this a book I have traditionally and self-published 10 novels. Mostly mysteries). They know I love camping and the beach, football, making art, and on and on. To them I'm a real person.

Tell them when they disappoint you. Tell the students when they make you sad. Tell them when you're angry or getting angry. Tell them when you're proud. Let them know when you're bursting with happiness. Confide in them when you're tired. Tell them when you're excited and hopeful. You have to spend a lot of time with your students. Be real.

Share your humanity with them. I'll bet they'll treat you more humanely.

HUMOR
(THEATRE OF
THE ABSURD)

I know that parts of this guide make me seem like a hard and heartless guy, but I assure you it all comes from a place of love. If you were to walk into my classroom unannounced, 9 out of 10 times you would find smiling, laughter, and all of us having a pretty good time as we work and enjoy each other's company. I think humor is my favorite and best tool for cracking those hard kids. Humor keeps the atmosphere light and when the students are in a good mood they're more likely to behave.

When I sense trouble on the horizon my first line of defense is oftentimes my warped sense of humor. I think I already mentioned I use different voices at times. I also do something that I call "theatre of the absurd." It's a trick I use to change what the student is thinking about. For example: A student comes into my class and is upset about something that happened earlier in the day. We've tried talking about it but can't seem to resolve the issue. The student just won't let it go. So, it's time to change what they're thinking about. I have lots of go to situations to choose from. One of my favorites is my wife's birthday. I tell the student my wife's birthday is coming up (it may be a long way off but this isn't a lie) and I need their advice on what to give her. This is when I tell them I'm thinking of buying her a chainsaw. They stop thinking of what has been bothering them all morning and try to figure out why in the world I would buy my wife a chainsaw. I play dumb and suggest maybe a shovel would be better. And we go from there—the student's thoughts have stopped thinking about their earlier problem for a moment and maybe you've even made them smile. I've had this conversation go off in many directions where we've planned a surprise party for her with jugglers, a cotton candy machine, and pony rides. We envision the perfect party and who doesn't like to think about parties? Theatre of the absurd!

A handful of the students don't celebrate Christmas at my school. One of my students who is easy to anger was sitting at a table with a couple of other kids talking about Christmas when I could tell his mood was getting dark. A perfect time for theatre of the absurd. I went over to the table and sat down with the 3 kids. I looked at the kid who doesn't celebrate Christmas and asked him if he wanted to know what I celebrated. He nodded and I told him I celebrate rock-and-roll. He smiled from ear to ear. I could tell by the way he looked at me that he knew I was kidding. I went on to tell the kids at the table something about drum sets, electric guitars, and grandmothers in mosh pits. I had to explain mosh pits and was glad to do so. All three of the kids were laughing when I left the table. I told them all to rock on as I walked away.

The trick here is to get the student thinking of something else. I have bits about the horse I ride to school, the helicopter on the roof, the pool in the school basement, and on and on. All you need for this to work is a starting point and a little bit of imagination.

POST WINTER BREAK AMNESIA

I can almost guarantee you that the students will forget all the rules over the winter break. Or at least it will seem that way. I take the first week back to reteach the rules and expectations. I teach them like it's the first of the year. I don't gloss over anything and assume they'll remember the rules. I go with the assumption they've forgotten them all. If you don't, it's going to be a long and grueling stretch until the end of the year. You'll be longing for that beach chair before February even rolls around.

It's a great time to redo the seating chart as well. It revitalizes me to see the faces in the room in a different way and it gives the students a fresh start as well. I don't move everybody because sometimes I've found some combinations that work pretty well, but I do move a lot of the students. I tell them that if I move them it doesn't mean they've done anything wrong, we're just doing some New Year rearranging.

I do the same thing after Spring Break and any other

long breaks during the school year. I may not always rearrange seats, but I always reteach the rules and expectations.

HAVE A CLASS MEETING

Sometimes I find it helps to have a class meeting to address certain behaviors. I call the students to the carpet and I sit down on the floor with them. I'm very serious. So, immediately they see something is different. I always teach standing up and I'm usually smiling and energetic. I tell them that we're having a class meeting to discuss something that's bothering me.

For example: I had a first grade class that loved to get out of their seats. In my classroom the students are responsible for getting out all the supplies and putting them away so there is some freedom to get up when needed. The expectation though is that you go right back to your seat. You don't take a lap around the room to say hello to all your friends and do two cartwheels across the carpet on your way back. But that's what was happening and no matter how many reminders I gave it continued to happen. So, we had a meeting. It wasn't a meeting where I raised all of my grievances. I only addressed the one

I wanted corrected more than any other. I spoke first and told them my concern. I asked for suggestions on why they thought it was happening and what they thought we could do to fix it. I gave them a voice. And then I put on their training wheels. I told them that for the remaining class period they were not allowed to get out of their seat without asking and telling me the reason. Was it annoying for me? Oh yeah. When somebody would ask to get something I would say yes and watch them get it and go right back to their seat. I only let one go at a time so I could watch. Did I mention it was annoying? And guess what? I did it again the next two times I saw them.

And then we had another class meeting. I thought they might be ready for me to take off their training wheels. I asked if they would like to be allowed to get out of their seats without having to ask. I asked what they would do. I asked what they would not do. I told them what I would do if it didn't work. And they did much, much better. They weren't perfect, but who is? There was one girl who didn't get it. She had to raise her hand to get out of her seat for a while longer, but it was only one hand going up, and not 25—not so annoying.

If you've never had a class meeting, give it a try. Give the students a voice. Get them thinking about whatever issue it is you're having, and then put on the training wheels if they're needed.

A FEW
OBSERVATIONS

I have the unique opportunity to teach 30 different classes each and every week. I get to see how 30 different teachers treat their classes and hear the things they say about them. I stand in the hall outside my room as the classes come down the hall. I'm on the end of a hall that seems to go on and on forever. I've joked at times that if I ever want to travel to the other side of the building I'd be smart to keep a pair of roller skates or a scooter in my room—it's that long. As the teachers come down the hall with their classes I observe how the teachers lead. Some teachers, I kid you not are on their phones and oblivious to children jumping up to slap the top of doorways, spinning, dancing, and all sorts of mischief. If they let the kids get away with this in public I wonder what it must be like behind closed doors in their classrooms. I would never correct another teacher in front of her class or say something to the class in a passive aggressive manner—it's not my style. I simply stop them at my door and tell them I'll wait until they are ready. Other teachers make empty threats. I hear one teacher yell at her class several times a week that if they continue to talk in the hall the entire class will miss recess. They are at recess every day. They know she doesn't mean business. Other teachers are sometimes late to my class because their classes could not get things together. These teachers mean business.

Many times I get to teach the same students 6 years in a row. One kid, I'll call him Teddy, was a holy terror in kindergarten. He made me reevaluate my career choice every time I came in contact with him. His kindergarten teacher couldn't stand him and I couldn't blame her. The next year in 1st grade he was lucky enough to have a teacher with a giant heart and mountains of patience. Teddy wasn't too bad in 1st grade and I chalked it up to him growing up. In 2nd grade his teacher was out of her league. She didn't know what to do with him and horribly behaved Teddy was back. In 3rd grade he had one of my favorite teachers in the school. She challenges the students, expects them to give their all, and loves them like they are her own. Teddy was a dream—the perfect student. This year he's in 4th grade and back to bad Teddy. A teacher's style matters. Teachers have the amazing ability to affect the way a child acts and this will in turn affect what he or she is able to learn that year.

Some teachers have great classes every year. Watch these teachers. Study these teachers.

Steal their ideas.

I do.

HAVING A BAD DAY

I'm a pretty happy-go-lucky guy, but like everybody else in this world I have the occasional bad day. On these days, things that usually don't bother me, or things that I'm usually able to ignore are impossible to tune out and I'm left on edge all day. Luckily I'm fairly self-aware and I have to remind myself all day that the students are being their normal selves, but I'm not my normal self. I remind myself that my sensitivity to noises is heightened. I tell myself over and over again that it's not them, it's me. I do my best to keep myself in check and to hold my tongue.

When you're having a bad day it's okay to tell the students. They won't all magically behave because you let them in on your secret, but maybe a handful of them will keep it in mind and give you a break. I tell my students. I might say something like, "I just want to let you all know that I'm not feeling my best today. I'm not going to have a lot of patience, so watch yourselves." I've put them on notice. They've been fairly warned. If somebody decides to test me I'll remind them of the black cloud hanging over my head.

You're allowed to have a bad day now and then. Try not to let it affect your responses to the students' misdeeds differently than on your normal days.

THE LETTER

I've used this method a dozen times and it always works. Let's say there's a student giving you trouble, and he or she won't come around to anything you say or any of the ideas you come up with as you're trying to deal with the situation. For these kids I write a letter to their parents, print it out, and I read it to them. The whole time I'm reading it to them they're shaking their head side to side and begging me not to send it home. In my letter I'm blunt and I'm ruthless. This is not a letter they want to go home. When I finish reading they beg me not to send it home. And that's when I make the deal.

"I'm going to give you one last chance to keep this letter from being sent to your house," I say. I walk over to my desk and I open my top drawer. I slip the letter inside and close the drawer. "I'm going to keep it in here for now. But, if we have any more problems, even one tiny problem, I'm going to pull the letter out of my drawer and send it to your house. You have the power to keep the letter in my drawer forever. It's up to you."

When those kids begin to misbehave I walk over to

my desk and I pull out the letter and I get an en-velope. That's usually all it takes. I had one kid who pushed me every week. I would be licking and seal-ing the envelope when he would finally give, but he always gave in and did what I said.

One of my friends also uses this method from time to time and she says it works wonders for her as well.

Give it a shot. I bet it'll work for you as well.

THE ROBOT

Some students don't know how to take no for an answer. They'll ask you the same thing over and over again, trying to break you down until you finally give up and change your mind. That's when I employ a strategy I call the robot.

Some students I've taught are certainly destined to be captains of the debate team. They can argue a point to death. It doesn't matter what I say, they will continue to argue. But, they don't last very long against the robot.

For example: I had one girl who didn't like her new assigned seat when we switched after break. She asked me if she could move and I said no. She asked a few more times and I continued to say no. She asked why and I answered. She said she was the only girl at a table with two boys. I looked around the room and proved that statement wrong. She tried a new approach. I tried to reason with her for a few more minutes and it wasn't working, so I turned into the robot. I wiped all expressions from my face and let emotion run out of my body. My answer from that point forward to whatever she said or asked was, "I said no." Although I didn't speak like a robot, my words were robotic. The words had no inflection. They were nothing but words. The same words. Over and over. No more arguing. My eyes were blank. And then I walked away. Whenever she tried to argue the point later I turned into the robot. "I said no."

It usually doesn't take too long for them to get the point if you don't break character.

TEACH KINDNESS

Kindness seems like a simple concept. I have to remind myself often that a lot of the kids I teach don't have a home life like I did growing up. Although my family was far from rich, I did have the luxury of having my mom home every day when I got home from school. My dad came home from work a few hours later and we all sat down for dinner at the same table every night. My parents taught me how to better myself and how to treat other people. I was also taught unconditional love.

Some families are just trying to survive. Children are left to fend for themselves and they might not have someone to teach them how to treat other people. They might not know what unconditional love feels like.

A lot of times as students are working on their projects, they will find that they don't have the color they need. So, they'll go over to one of the other tables and take what they need. This, of course causes a problem as the people from the table in which they took the marker or crayon feel slighted. So, instead of getting on to the person who took it,

I teach them the right way to do it. I demonstrate how you go over to the table, explain your problem, and ask if you may borrow an item. I teach them to say thank you. And more often than not, they will smile and I can tell that this never occurred to them, but they are delighted with the method. It always fills me with joy the next time I see them do it without my assistance.

Some of the things that may seem so simple to the rest of us need to be taught to the kids in your classroom. I teach my students the value of being considerate. I teach them that no matter what they do, they are still worthy.

Teach kindness.

Teach unconditional love.

Teach your students to be better humans.

PEER PRESSURE

I'm pretty sure we were all taught growing up that peer pressure is a bad thing. But what if I told you that I use it in my classroom to get some students to behave. Would you think I was a bad person? It's harmless when used the right way.

Let's face it, we've all been a part of a group at one time or another that didn't get to do something that we wanted because somebody angered the person in charge. It's a part of life.

While the kids are working in my class they are allowed to whisper. If the whispering gets too loud I say "Strike 1" and it's their first warning that the noise level is too high. I give them 3 strikes and after the third we have 5 minutes of silent art. The students may not talk or get out of their seats for the 5 minutes. Sometimes there are certain tables that are loud while everyone else is doing the right thing. In this situation I might say, "Table 2, you just got your class a strike. You're going to have a lot of people disappointed in you if they don't get to whisper with their friends just because you aren't following the rules." Table 2 will look around the room to find 20 other children giving them the death stare.

Now, I won't take away something big with peer pressure. That's not fair for the whole class and I don't want somebody to get a beat down at recess for their bad choices. I only want them to feel a little uncomfortable. For example, I wouldn't tell a whole class they didn't get to have recess because one kid was being a clown. The clown might not get to do it, but I wouldn't use the peer pressure method in that manner.

JUST TAKE A DAY OFF

You probably won't read this in the employee handbook, but every once in a while you just have to take the day off and get away from it all. One of my aunts taught for 30 years and when I asked her what she would do differently with her career she said, "I would have taken more days off."

And I have taken that to heart. It may sound excessive to you, but if I'm not sick I take one day off a month. Some call it a mental health day—I just call it the secret to my sanity. If I happen to be sick that month and need a real sick day I don't do it because I don't want to be out too much. I'm not *that* guy.

In the county where I work we get 5 personal days after 10 years of service and I use them for these days mixed in with the sick days. I have some teacher friends who never take sick days and they never take their personal days either. I could understand this if it was possible to save the days up and retire a year early, but it doesn't work that way in my district.

This school year Thursday is my hardest day. I have a couple of students who make me want to pull my hair out. It's rare that I can't figure a kid out but I have two in the same 5th grade class. I dread Thursdays. I've decided that in 3 weeks I'm going to use one of my personal days on Thursday. It gives me something to look forward to. The next two weeks when I see my two knuckleheads I'll have a little more patience knowing I'm going to get a break from them. It'll be my secret weapon.

Do yourself a favor and every now and then stay home and relax. Get your mind right. It will be worth it in the end to both you and your students.

DON'T PUNISH YOURSELF

Early in my career I sometimes said things in anger before actually thinking them through. I've since learned to slow myself down and to gather my thoughts before speaking. I've learned to not take things personally. I've developed a countenance in which I don't feel much anger. I may feel disappointment or confusion with certain behaviors, but anger leads to bad decisions and with bad decisions we oftentimes punish ourselves.

I've mentioned several times in this guide that I don't like calling parents. I know many, many teachers who don't have a problem with it at all, but I do. I don't like it. I might even hate it. I only want to call parents as a last resort. And by last resort I mean the last, last, last resort. So, it's not a consequence I give very often. I probably make 2 phone calls a year. Early in my career it was my go-to move, said in anger. I hadn't done anything wrong and I ended up feeling like I was the one who was punished. My wrongdoing was my mouth getting ahead of my head.

I can remember a teacher who our school chewed up and spit out threatening her class as she came down the hall that if they said one more word they would lose their recess. I saw this happen more than once. I'd watch her, shaking her finger in the air, eyes wild with fury. Somebody would say another word and she'd take away their recess. This lady needed a break from these children. She needed them to run wild outside and release some of their energy. She didn't need to trap herself inside a room with them for 30 minutes. She certainly punished the class, but she also punished herself.

I once had a class that could not stop talking to save their lives. I had the great idea that I would shock them into compliance by not doing an art project one day. When they walked in the room I had the art textbooks, which had never been opened or taken out of the cabinet sitting on their tables. There were questions to answer, pages to read, and essays to complete. It took me a long time to create the packet. I punished myself with extra work. It took *forever* to grade. Double punishment for me. Were they shocked? Yes. But so was I with my poor choice of consequences.

When you're coming up with consequences for students or classes, make sure you're not punishing yourself and don't punish when you're angry. You'll probably regret it.

END OF THE YEAR

Some teachers ease up on their rules toward the end of the year. They do the same the week before winter break and spring break. Not me—in my classroom it's business as usual every day—even on the last day of the school year.

As an art teacher I teach some students for 6 years. If I throw the rules out the window on this day and on that day, what does that tell them? It tells them that the rules are not always important. I may seem like a dullard and a party pooper, but consistency always matters. And, they will remember.

The end of the year is hard because a great majority of teachers will loosen up. Kids will take every inch you give them. I think some teachers already have one flip-flop on the beach because some classes are wild. Getting them back to normal can be hard, but it's possible.

My friend across the hall and I think the same and it helps the mission of staying normal when you have others on your side. When students come down the hall toward our rooms they know that it's business as usual. We wait outside our rooms with our game faces on. So, when it gets to the end of the year, speak up, and recruit others to keep it normal. Are my friend and I ready for the lazy days by the pool? You better believe it but do yourself and your students a favor and keep it normal.

Another thing to keep in mind is that some students will act out toward the end of the year because school is their safe place. It might be the only place they know for a fact that they will get fed consistently. Maybe their parents leave them alone in the summer for long stretches of time with nothing to do. Not all kids love summer. For whatever reason it may be, some students are terrified of the idea of being away from school for two months. So, be aware that some of the acting out and negative behaviors toward the end of the year may stem from this.

Do yourself and the other teachers around you a favor and keep things normal at the end of the year.

TELL THEM WHY

One of my rules is to enter the room silently. I don't do this because I'm not a nice guy who doesn't like kids to enjoy their time at school. I do it because I don't want to start each class asking the students to be quiet. I want to get right to the lesson so we can use our time wisely. A silent start sets the tone for a calm and productive class period. There is time to talk later.

One time when the students were entering the room and I reminded them of the rule I heard a voice say, "Why?" It was an eye-opening moment. I was asking them to do something and they didn't even know why.

So now, when I introduce a rule, I tell the students the reasoning behind the rule. Even kindergarten students can understand the concepts.

You don't have to have an in-depth discussion about society and laws although I have had a few students who took the conversation there.

Keep it simple. Explain why you have your rules and if you can't think of a reason then maybe you need to rethink the rule.

I'M NOT MEAN,
I'M STRICT

I was called mean by a kindergartener years and years ago. As I was making my way around the room I came up behind him as he was breaking crayons in half and putting them back in the box. I asked him what he was doing and he of course said, "Nothing." It seems to be a pretty popular answer when you catch a kid in the act of doing something wrong. I sat down next to him and asked him a question. I asked, "If I came to your house, do you think I would break your stuff?" He shook his head. I told him he couldn't use my crayons, markers, or anything other than a pencil for the rest of the day. I told him he couldn't use them the next time he came either. If we happened to be painting the next time he came, he would use a pencil. If we were using oil pastels, he would use a pencil. And that's when he called me mean.

I walked away to put up the crayons and thought about what he said. I circled back and sat down again to tell him that I'm not mean, I'm strict. I explained the difference in words he could understand. I asked him if I should call his mom to explain the difference. He was adamant that I should *not* call his mom to explain the difference. I asked him if I should call his dad to explain the difference between mean and strict. He again said no with great animation. We made a deal and he assured me he would explain it all to his parents so I wouldn't have to. I have a feeling he may have forgotten or decided not to and that was okay. My hope was that he didn't forget the difference between mean and strict.

I'm a human being so I'm sure from time to time I can be mean. But it's rare. Very rare. Mean in my own words is to act with hate in your heart. A mean person belittles another. I don't do that—I'm strict. Strict in my own words is to be incredibly direct. Strict is not looking the other way when kids break the rules. Strict is taking action every time. Strict is sticking to the rules I've made without ever wavering. Strict is tough love.

I'm not mean.

I'm strict.

TALL TALES

I saved this strategy for last because you might not agree with this one. I don't like to think that I lie to my students, so I think of this strategy as using fables or something similar for a positive outcome.

Since I've been teaching for nearly two decades I have a lot of stories. When I have a class that is not behaving I will tell them about another class I had years ago and what happened to them when they acted in the same manner. I tend to base these stories somewhat on reality but then my imaginative mind and skill at exaggeration takes over to spin the whole thing into a tall tale. The story might be about a whole class or an individual. At the end of my tale I always advise the class how they might avoid the same horrible outcome and learn from the past.

One year I made up a fake student and even gave him a name. His name was Junior. When I introduced a project I would sometimes tell them how Junior did it. Junior, of course, always did it wrong, but it allowed me to point out in a humorous way how *not* to do a project. But, I soon discovered that

I had created a bit of a problem for myself because the students always wanted to hear about Junior. Whenever we did anything they wanted to hear how Junior did it. How did Junior wash his hands? How did Junior use the scissors? How did Junior line up? It was exhausting. Maybe I deserved it for being a big liar.

Tall tales can be an effective strategy if you can find a happy medium and don't feel too guilty about blurring the truth.

YOU GOT THIS

Thank you. Thank you for reading my guide and thank you for having the guts to get up every day to teach. It isn't easy, but it's worth it. Kids are worth your energy and your dedication.

Please take my ideas and make them your own. It is my hope that you will find a few of them that will make your life easier. I hope that reading this will help you know that there are thousands and thousands of teachers out there in the same position as you. You're not alone. Teaching is hard. Classroom management is something that must be learned over time with your experiences. Believe me, every year it gets easier if you make the effort to improve. And I know you will.

I believe in you.

You got this.

57011498R00062

Made in the USA
Columbia, SC
04 May 2019